Text copyright © 2021 by Lizzie DeYoung Charbonneau
Illustrations copyright © 2021 by Misha Iver

All rights reserved

LCCN 2021910084
ISBN 978-1-955619-02-8

Publisher's Cataloging-in-Publication Data

Names: Charbonneau, Lizzie DeYoung, 1987– author. | Iver, Misha, 1990– illustrator.

Title: Your whole body : from your head to your toes, and everything in between! / written by Lizzie DeYoung Charbonneau ; illustrated by Misha Iver.

Description: First edition. | Medford, Massachusetts : Arctic Flower Publishing, [2021] | Audience: ages 2–6. | Summary: "Your Whole Body: From Your Head to Your Toes and Everything in Between!" is a diverse, gender inclusive, and ability inclusive book for young children about the entire body, explaining and illustrating all of the major body parts including the genitals.--Publisher.

Identifiers: ISBN: 978-1-955619-00-4 (hardback) | 978-1-955619-02-8 (paperback) | 978-1-955619-01-1 (ebook) | LCCN: 2021910084

Subjects: LCSH: Human body--Juvenile literature. | Human anatomy--Juvenile literature. | Human physiology--Juvenile literature. | Children's questions and answers--Juvenile literature. | CYAC: Human body. | Human anatomy. | Human physiology. | Human biology. | LCGFT: Anatomical atlases. | Instructional and educational works.

Classification: LCC: QM27 .C53 2021 | DDC: 612--dc23

Arctic Flower Publishing
Medford, Massachusetts 02155

Visit us at www.arcticflowerpublishing.com

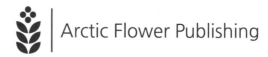

YOUR WHOLE BODY

From your head to your toes, and EVERYTHING in between!

Written by **Lizzie DeYoung Charbonneau**
Illustrated by **Misha Iver**

Your **BODY** is amazing!
Let's explore—

FROM YOUR HEAD TO YOUR TOES,
AND EVERYTHING IN BETWEEN!

On top of your head, you may have **HAIR**. Hair helps your head stay warm when the weather is cold and cool when the weather is hot.

There are lots of colors and textures of hair.
Some people have light hair.
Some people have dark hair.
Some people have straight hair.
Some people have curly hair.
Some people have no hair.

SHAFT

ROOT

SCALP

On the sides of your head are your **EARS**. You use your ears to hear sounds, like leaves rustling in the wind and birds chirping on a summer day.

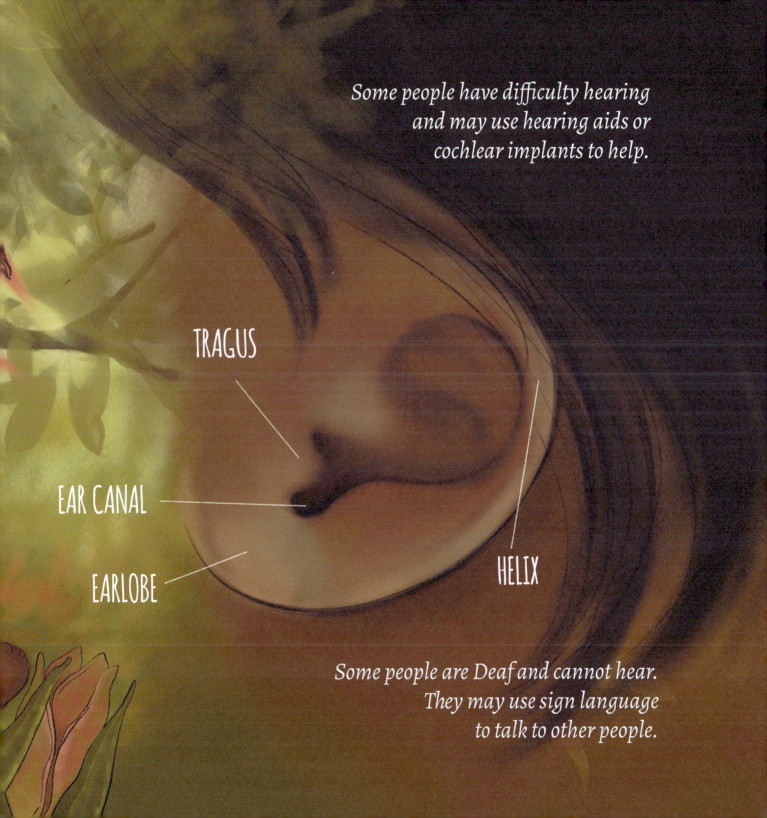

Next is your **FACE**! The movements you make with your face can show people how you are feeling, like when you are happy, sad, silly, or mad.

The face has 43 muscles that help show your feelings!

FOREHEAD
EYEBROW
TEMPLE
CHEEK
JAW
CHIN

Your **EYES** let you see. You can see the clouds in the sky, your friends' smiles, and the words in your favorite book.

*There are many shapes and shades of eyes.
Some eyes are round. Some are narrow.
Some tear ducts are hidden. Some you can see.
Some eyelids are creased. Some are smooth.
Some irises are dark. Some are light.*

Some people have difficulty seeing and may use glasses or contact lenses to see more clearly.

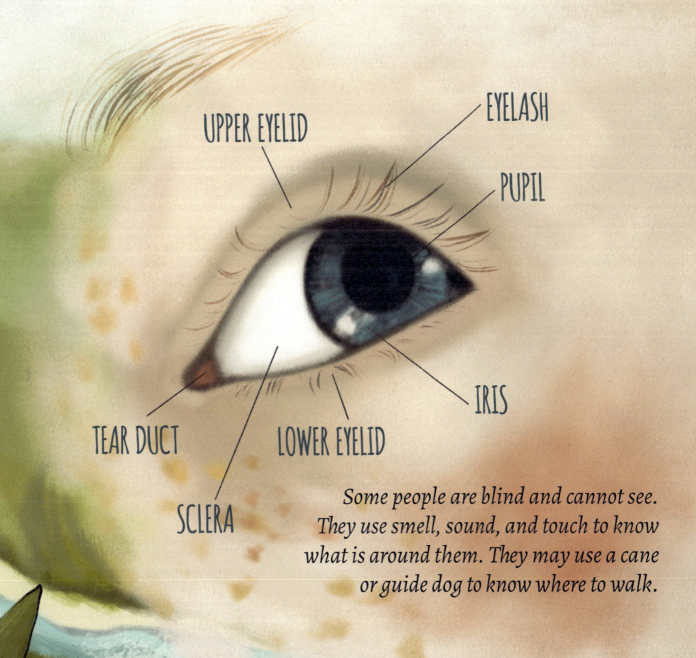

UPPER EYELID
EYELASH
PUPIL
IRIS
LOWER EYELID
TEAR DUCT
SCLERA

Some people are blind and cannot see. They use smell, sound, and touch to know what is around them. They may use a cane or guide dog to know where to walk.

Your **NOSE** lets you smell scents,
like flowers in a garden and grass after the rain.

Smell is directly connected to what you remember and how you feel about it.

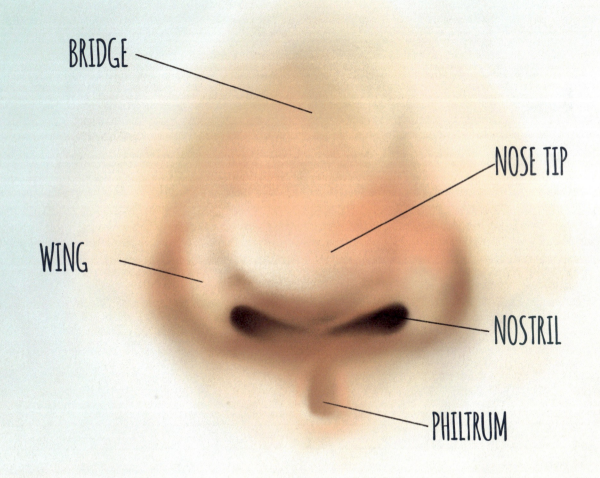

BRIDGE

NOSE TIP

WING

NOSTRIL

PHILTRUM

You breathe through your nose and **MOUTH**.
You also use your mouth to eat, speak, and smile!

When you eat, your teeth chew your food, and your tongue tastes your food and helps you swallow.

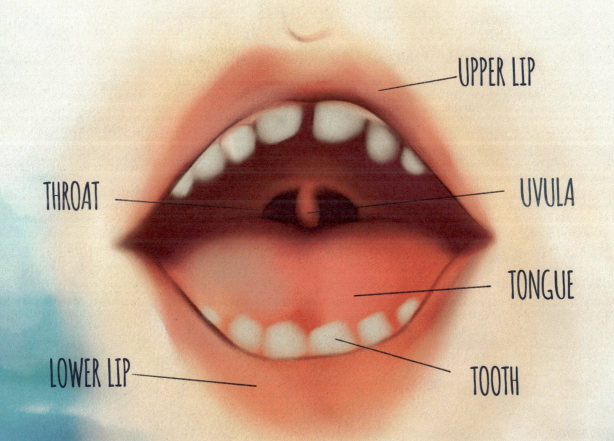

UPPER LIP

THROAT

UVULA

TONGUE

LOWER LIP

TOOTH

When you speak, your lips and tongue make different shapes to create words.

Some people feel pain in their joints when the weather changes.

Your **CHEST** is where air goes in and out of your body. When you breathe in, your chest gets bigger. When you breathe out, your chest gets smaller.

CLAVICLE

JUGULAR NOTCH

ARMPIT

RIBS

NIPPLE

Many people can hold their breath for up to 90 seconds. Some people can hold their breath even longer!

Some people grow breasts when they get older. Breasts and nipples can be used to feed babies.

You touch and hold things with your **HANDS** using your **FINGERS** and **THUMBS**. Your hands help you draw a picture, solve a puzzle, and hold someone else's hand.

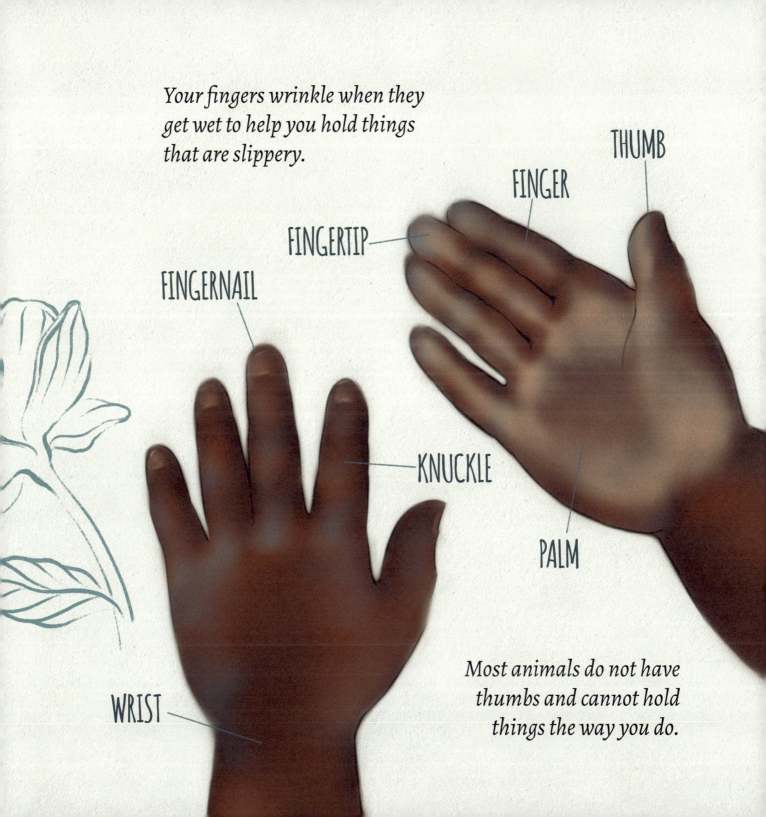

Your fingers wrinkle when they get wet to help you hold things that are slippery.

THUMB
FINGER
FINGERTIP
FINGERNAIL
KNUCKLE
PALM
WRIST

Most animals do not have thumbs and cannot hold things the way you do.

ARMS help you move your hands where they need to go. Together, your arms and your hands help you climb rocks, build forts, and swing on the monkey bars. You can also use your arms to hug someone you love!

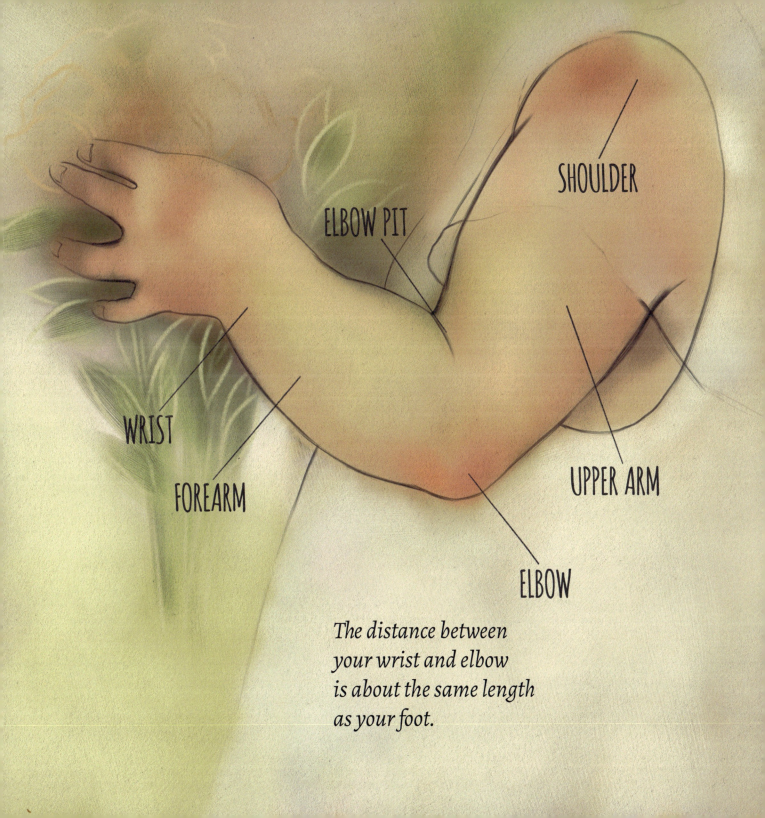

Your **ABDOMEN** is where food goes after you swallow it. Food helps your body go!

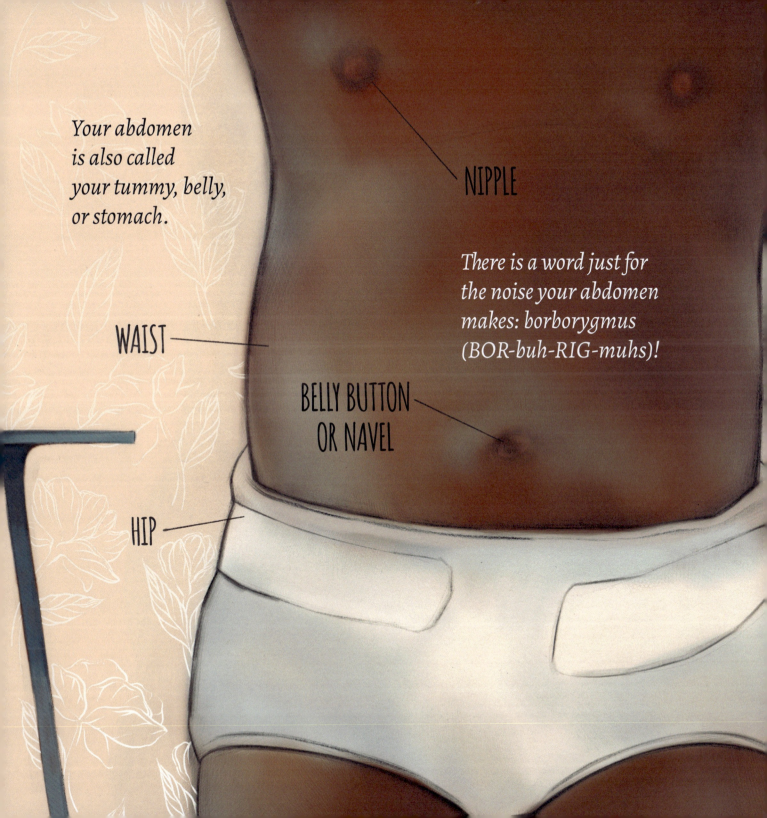

Your abdomen is also called your tummy, belly, or stomach.

NIPPLE

There is a word just for the noise your abdomen makes: borborygmus (BOR-buh-RIG-muhs)!

WAIST

BELLY BUTTON OR NAVEL

HIP

After your body is done with the food you ate, what is left over becomes feces and urine. Feces leave your body through your **ANUS**. Urine leaves your body through your **URETHRA**.

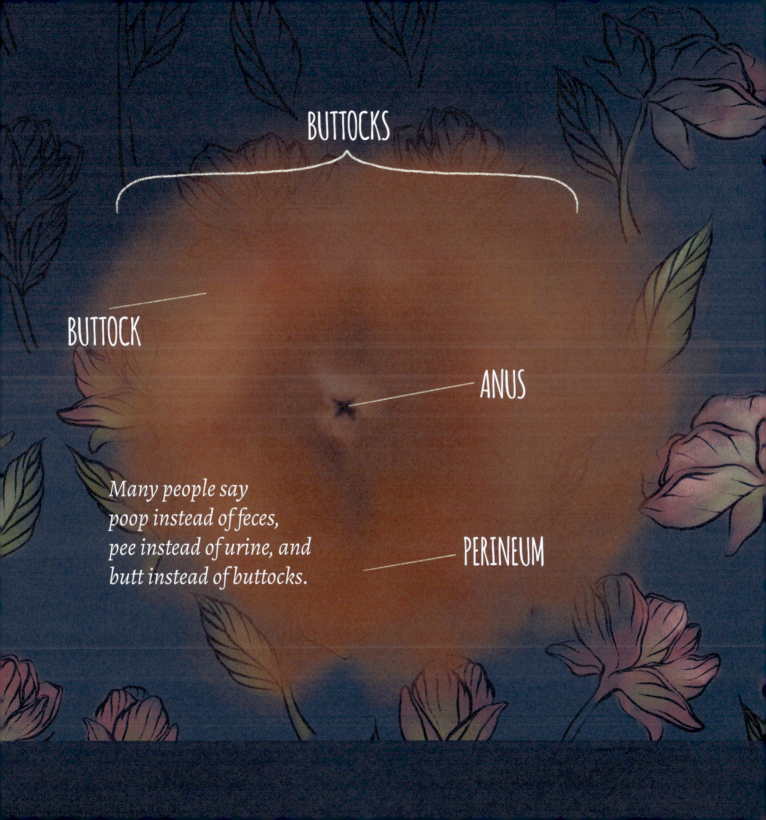

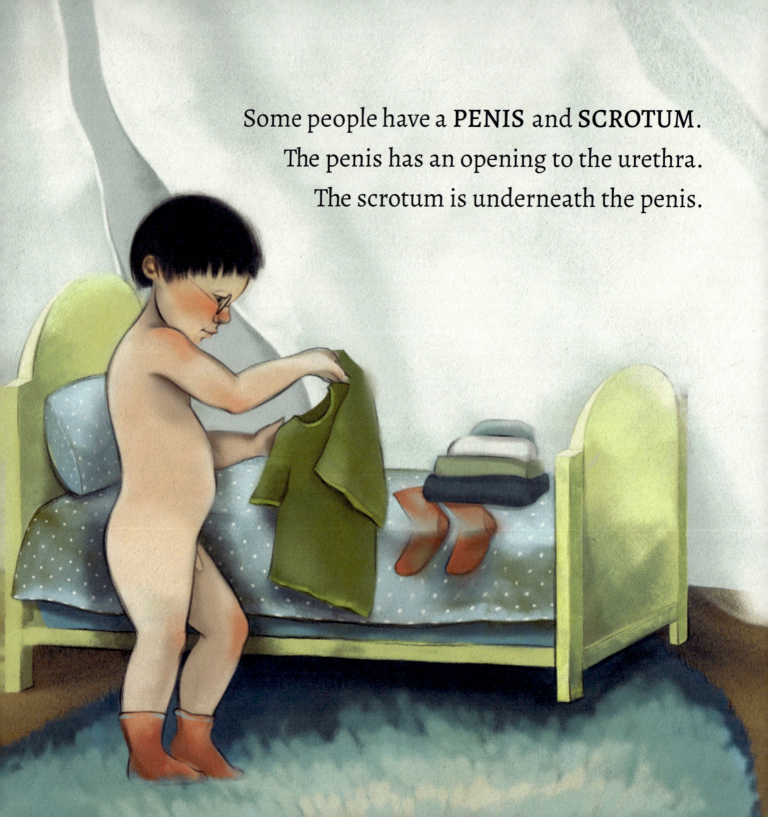

Some people have a **PENIS** and **SCROTUM**.
The penis has an opening to the urethra.
The scrotum is underneath the penis.

Some people have skin, called foreskin, that covers the top of their penis. Some people are circumcised and have had the foreskin removed.

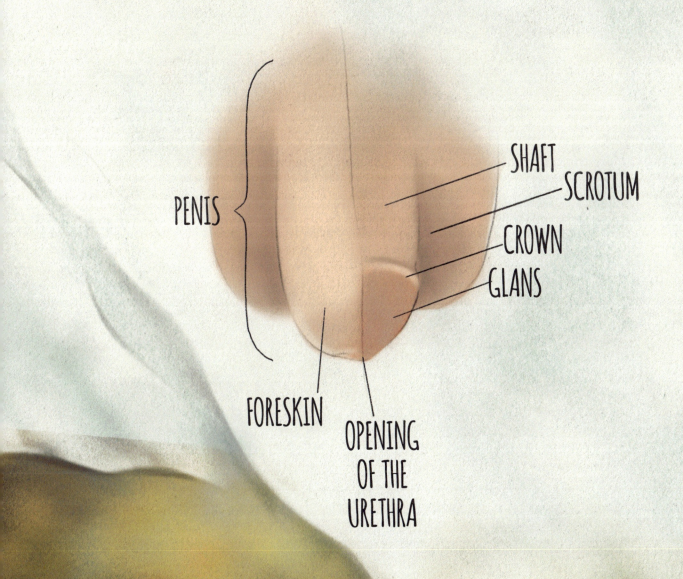

Some people have a **VULVA**. The vulva includes the labia, the clitoris, an opening to the urethra, and an opening to the vagina.

Some people say vagina when they mean vulva. The vagina is on the inside of the body, and the vulva is on the outside.

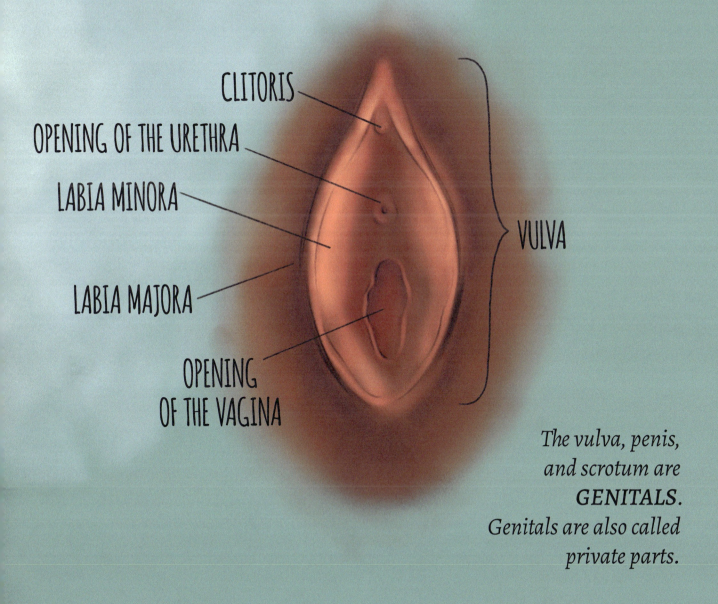

The vulva, penis, and scrotum are **GENITALS**. Genitals are also called private parts.

Your **LEGS** help your body move. You can use your legs to take a walk in the park, run a race, and kick a ball!

Some people have difficulty moving their legs, and some people cannot move their legs. They may use braces, crutches, a walker, a cane, or a wheelchair to move around.

THIGH

CALF

KNEE

SHIN

Your **FEET** are what you stand on. They are at the ends of your legs. At the ends of your feet are your **TOES**, which help you stay balanced so you do not fall over.

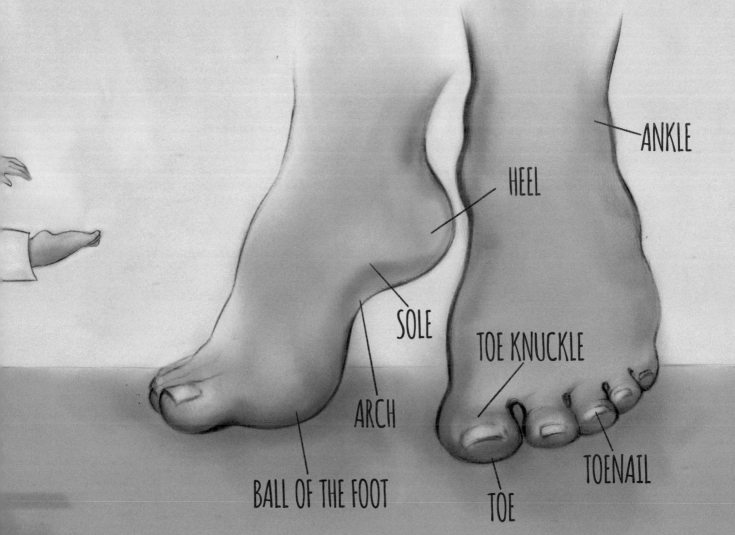

Many people have one foot that is a little bigger than the other foot.

All the parts of your body work together
to make you who you are.
From your head to your toes,
your body is amazing!

For Colin, my amazing dancing astronaut! —LDC
For Lana and Forest—the two biggest loves of my life! —MI

This book could not have been made without the support of many wonderful people! We would like to give a special thanks to Clare Boersma, Clare Hurley, and Jan and Don DeYoung. Thank you!

Did you know?

Knowing the proper names for genitals is a critical body safety skill for young children.

Learn more body safety skills with the FREE Body Safety Rules download.

Get yours now at resources.arcticflowerpublishing.com/bodysafetyrules

Lizzie DeYoung Charbonneau is a children's book author, software developer, and mother. Lizzie grew up in Anchorage, Alaska, and currently resides in Massachusetts.

Lizzie believes it is important for young children to know the names of all of their body parts. To help teach her son about his body, Lizzie looked for a picture book that discussed genitals the same way as other body parts. She wasn't able to find one, so she decided to write it, consulting with parents, child safety experts, pediatricians, gender specialists, and educators. The result is *Your Whole Body*, an inclusive book for children about the entire body.

To learn more, visit
arcticflowerpublishing.com.

Misha Iver is an illustrator who has made her home in Burlington, Vermont.

Because she believes that children's literature represents inspiration, transformation, and hope, she feels lucky to work in this field where she can be a part of a significant and beautiful force.

Misha Iver draws her deepest inspiration from nature, and her love for botanical illustration has made it a specialty of hers.

You can connect with Misha at
mishaiver.com

Printed in France by Amazon
Brétigny-sur-Orge, FR